P9-DHF-315

DATE DUE			

937
AME

Amery, Heather.

The time traveller
book of Rome and
Romans.

20034

MICHAEL T. SIMMONS ELEMENTARY

The Time Traveller Book of ROME AND ROMANS

Heather Amery and Patricia Vanags

Illustrated by Stephen Cartwright and Designed by John Jamieson

Contents

2   Going Back in Time

3   The People You Will Meet

4   On the Road to Rome

6   In the Streets of Rome

8   Petronius at Home

10   Going to School

12   Shops and Markets

14   Afternoon at the Baths

16   Gladiators and Charioteers

18   Building in the City

20   Petronius Gives a Feast

22   Summer in the Country

24   Marcus Joins the Army

26   Attacking a Citadel

28   The Roman Empire

30   The Story of Rome

32   Index and Further Reading

Going Back in Time

This is a book for everyone who would like to travel back in time. We have invented a Magic Time Travelling Helmet to help you. The trip to ancient Rome is nearly 2,000 years long but with the Helmet it takes seconds.

You may often have wanted to go to places you have read about in history; to see how people lived without all the things you know about—cars, television, telephones, jets and electric lights. In museums you can see some of the odd things they used. But museums cannot show you it all in one place. Below you can see how the Helmet works and on the next page are the people you will meet when you are wearing it.

Put on the Helmet

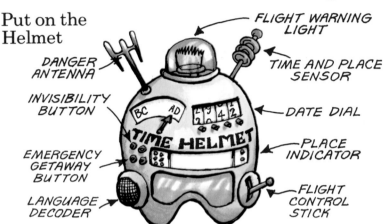

FLIGHT WARNING LIGHT

TIME AND PLACE SENSOR

DANGER ANTENNA

INVISIBILITY BUTTON

DATE DIAL

EMERGENCY GETAWAY BUTTON

PLACE INDICATOR

LANGUAGE DECODER

FLIGHT CONTROL STICK

TIME HELMET

This is your Magic Time Travelling Helmet. You can see it has lots of useful buttons for understanding foreign languages, for flying, for being invisible, and for a quick escape back to home.

Pick your Destination

This is where you are going. Set the 'Place' dial to 'Rome' and the 'Time' dial to 'A.D. 100'.

Below are a few stop-offs to give you an idea of how different things look when you jump back in time.

1940

Here we are in Northwest Europe at about the time your dad was born.

Things have not changed very much but notice the aeroplane and old radio.

1900

After a jump of 40 years, things have changed a lot. There is a gas lamp, no electricity, a funny telephone and a lot of decorated furniture.

1600

Back another 300 years and the room is lit by candles. Notice the small window with little panes of glass. There is a big log fire in the fireplace.

1200

Now we are at the time when people live in big, cold castles. There is no chimney for the fire, nor glass in the windows. Next stop—ancient Rome

The People You Will Meet

Everyone you will meet in this book lives in Rome. It is the capital of a great empire.

The rich people have pleasant, easy lives with lots of slaves to do all the work.

The poor people work hard to earn enough to eat. But the rich people give them cheap bread.

PETRONIUS

LIVIA

Petronius is a rich nobleman who lives in a large, comfortable house in Rome. He is a lawyer and an important official in the government. Petronius is a kind man who loves his wife, Livia, and his five children.

Livia married Petronius when she was only 12 years old. Her father chose her husband for her and gave Petronius' family a large sum of money, called a dowry. Livia looks after the house and has many slaves.

MARCUS

Marcus, Petronius' eldest son, is 16 years old. He is training to be a soldier in the Roman army. Like all children, even grown-up ones, he has to obey his father and ask his permission before he does anything.

CORNELIA

Cornelia, the eldest daughter, is 14 and is engaged to a young nobleman. Until her wedding, she lives at home, helping her mother in the house.

Claudia, the second daughter, is 12 and lives at home too. She has finished her schooling and now her mother is teaching her to spin and weave. A tutor gives her music and singing lessons.

CLAUDIA

Marius, the second son, is 15, and is learning about his father's business. When he is older, he will serve in the army for a while, like Marcus.

MARIUS

CAIUS

Caius, the youngest, is eight and goes to school every day. He does not like the Greek schoolmaster and would rather play with his friends.

AUNT ANTONIA

Petronius' sister, Antonia, and her two children, live with the family. Her husband was killed while fighting with the army. Now her brother gives her a home and looks after her.

Sestius, Petronius' cousin, lives in a city far from Rome. He is visiting the family to ask for Petronius' help with some legal business.

SESTIUS   BUSINESSMEN

Business men come to Petronius for his advice, to beg for favours and to borrow money. Some also come to do favours for him.

Pericles is secretary to Petronius. He is Greek and was a slave but he works so well, Petronius has given him his freedom and a special place in the household.

PERICLES

RICH FRIENDS

Rich and important friends of Petronius are invited to his dinner parties. Some are army officers and government officials.

SHOPKEEPERS

Poor shopkeepers and craftsmen work hard to make a living. Some are slaves who have bought their freedom. They live in crowded blocks of flats in the city.

SLAVES

The slaves in Petronius' house are captured foreigners who were bought at the slave market. If they run away, they may be beaten or put to death. But Petronius and Livia are kind to them. They are allowed to marry and have children. If they work hard, they may save up enough to buy their freedom.

On the Road to Rome

With the help of your Time Helmet, you have rushed back through nearly 2,000 years. It is A.D. 100. You are in Italy and on the road to Rome—the city away at the top of the picture.

Rome is now the biggest and most splendid city in the world. About 700 years before this time, it was a small village of wooden huts on one of the seven hills. Slowly the city has grown and fine stone houses, temples and public buildings have been built on all the hills.

As the city has grown bigger and richer, more people have come to live here. They have left their homes in the country and have learned to do all sorts of work.

The Romans have built good roads from their city so that their huge armies can march quickly along them. Look round you and see the people who travel to Rome. Turn over the page and you will be in the city itself.

Hunters have been shooting wild boar in the woods. Now they have stopped to cook meat over a fire.

At this tavern, travellers can buy food and drink and get a bed for the night. But they have to watch out for thieves who try to rob them.

TOMBSTONES

WINE JARS

A horseman carries official letters from the army commander in Britain to the emperor in Rome.

Milestones along the road mark out the distance to the middle of Rome in Roman miles.

ROAD MENDERS

This is Sestius who is going to stay with his cousin Petronius. Letters can take months to cross the empire so he visits Rome himself to settle a legal matter.

The paved roads are for fast traffic and important people. The slow farmcarts and poor people use the muddy tracks on each side.

Tombstones along the road mark the graves of people from Rome. No one is allowed to be buried inside the city boundaries.

4

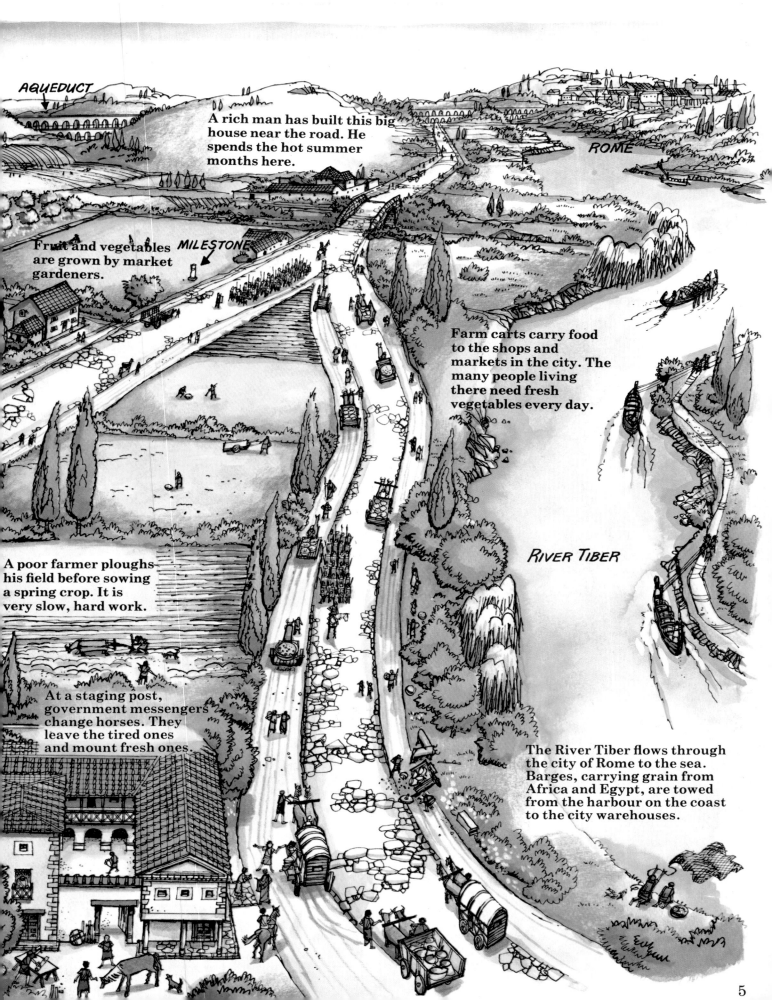

AQUEDUCT

A rich man has built this big house near the road. He spends the hot summer months here.

ROME

Fruit and vegetables are grown by market gardeners. **MILESTONE**

Farm carts carry food to the shops and markets in the city. The many people living there need fresh vegetables every day.

A poor farmer ploughs his field before sowing a spring crop. It is very slow, hard work.

RIVER TIBER

At a staging post, government messengers change horses. They leave the tired ones and mount fresh ones.

The River Tiber flows through the city of Rome to the sea. Barges, carrying grain from Africa and Egypt, are towed from the harbour on the coast to the city warehouses.

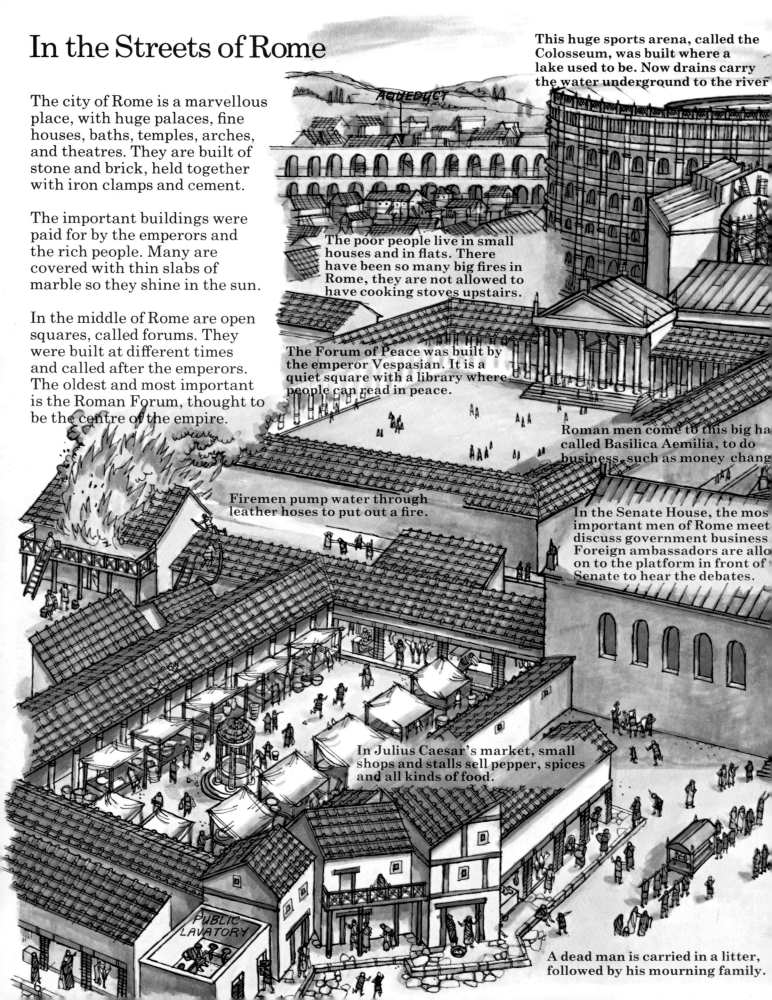

In the Streets of Rome

The city of Rome is a marvellous place, with huge palaces, fine houses, baths, temples, arches, and theatres. They are built of stone and brick, held together with iron clamps and cement.

The important buildings were paid for by the emperors and the rich people. Many are covered with thin slabs of marble so they shine in the sun.

In the middle of Rome are open squares, called forums. They were built at different times and called after the emperors. The oldest and most important is the Roman Forum, thought to be the centre of the empire.

AQUEDUCT

This huge sports arena, called the Colosseum, was built where a lake used to be. Now drains carry the water underground to the river

The poor people live in small houses and in flats. There have been so many big fires in Rome, they are not allowed to have cooking stoves upstairs.

The Forum of Peace was built by the emperor Vespasian. It is a quiet square with a library where people can read in peace.

Roman men come to this big ha called Basilica Aemilia, to do business, such as money chang

Firemen pump water through leather hoses to put out a fire.

In the Senate House, the mos important men of Rome meet discuss government business Foreign ambassadors are allo on to the platform in front of Senate to hear the debates.

In Julius Caesar's market, small shops and stalls sell pepper, spices and all kinds of food.

PUBLIC LAVATORY

A dead man is carried in a litter, followed by his mourning family.

The empire is now so strong and safe, the city does not need walls to protect it from enemies. New houses and flats have been built far outside the old city walls.

The glittering white and gold palace has been made larger and more magnificent by the emperors. No ordinary people are allowed inside the garden walls.

This arch was put up by Augustus, the first emperor of Rome and the nephew of Julius Caesar. Lots of emperors had arches like this one built to celebrate their victories.

In the round temple, called the Temple of the Vestals, a fire burns all the time. It is looked after by young priestesses.

AMBASSADORS

TEMPLE OF CAESAR

SACRED WAY

THIEF

A procession of family and friends leads a bride to the house of the bridegroom on her wedding day.

Priests and officials lead animals to be sacrificed. When they have cut an animal open, an expert will look at its insides. From them, the Romans believe, he can tell if the gods favour them in battle.

This platform, called the New Rostra, is used by public speakers when talking to the people in the Forum.

7

Petronius at Home

This is where Petronius lives with his family, his sister, and his slaves and servants. Petronius is rich and an important man in Rome. His house is large and comfortable, although you would think it is rather bare of furniture and cold in the winter. There are stone floors and open roofs.

Like all Roman fathers, Petronius is the master of his household. Everyone has to obey him. But he is kind and treats his slaves and servants well. When he wants a new slave, he buys one at the market. The slaves are captured foreigners and may have a high price if they are young, healthy and skilful.

The Romans get up very early in the morning, usually before it is light, even in summer. Petronius does not go out to work but stays at home. Men come to see him to discuss their problems, borrow money or ask a favour. Important business men come to give favours and advice.

These stairs lead up to the bedrooms which are lit by smokey oil lamps at night.

Livia and her daughter, Cornelia, are still in their bedroom. Their servants are helping them to do their hair and put on their make-up and jewellery. When they are ready, they will go out to visit friends.

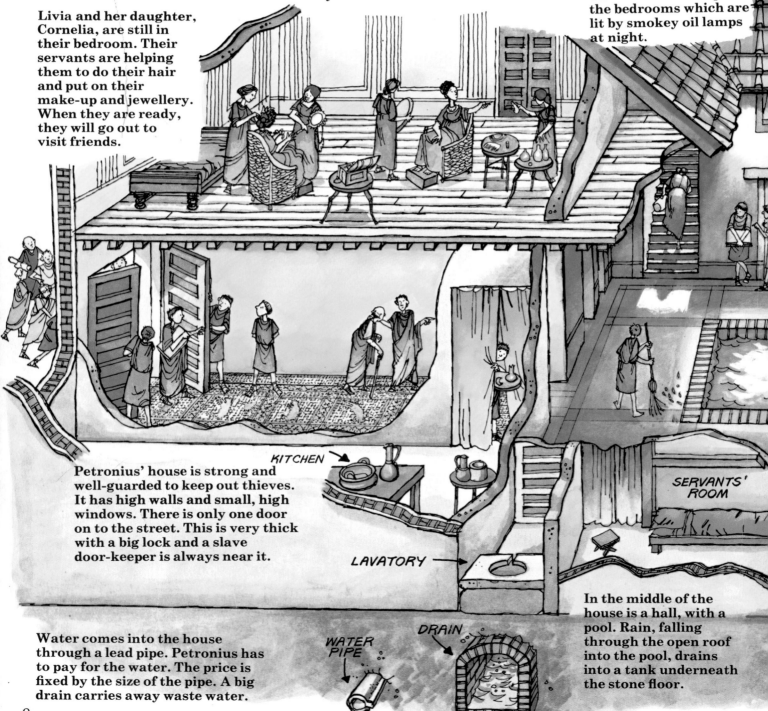

KITCHEN

SERVANTS' ROOM

Petronius' house is strong and well-guarded to keep out thieves. It has high walls and small, high windows. There is only one door on to the street. This is very thick with a big lock and a slave door-keeper is always near it.

LAVATORY

In the middle of the house is a hall, with a pool. Rain, falling through the open roof into the pool, drains into a tank underneath the stone floor.

Water comes into the house through a lead pipe. Petronius has to pay for the water. The price is fixed by the size of the pipe. A big drain carries away waste water.

WATER PIPE

DRAIN

Poor visitors have to wait for a long time in the hall or stand in a queue outside the front door. Important visitors are seen at once. When everyone has gone, Petronius will go out to see his friends or deal with a legal matter. He will also spend some time at the law courts.

Before Petronius sees the visitors, he puts on his toga. A slave carefully arranges the folds of the heavy woollen material. Only free citizens of Rome are allowed to wear togas. Petronius puts his on only for formal and state occasions.

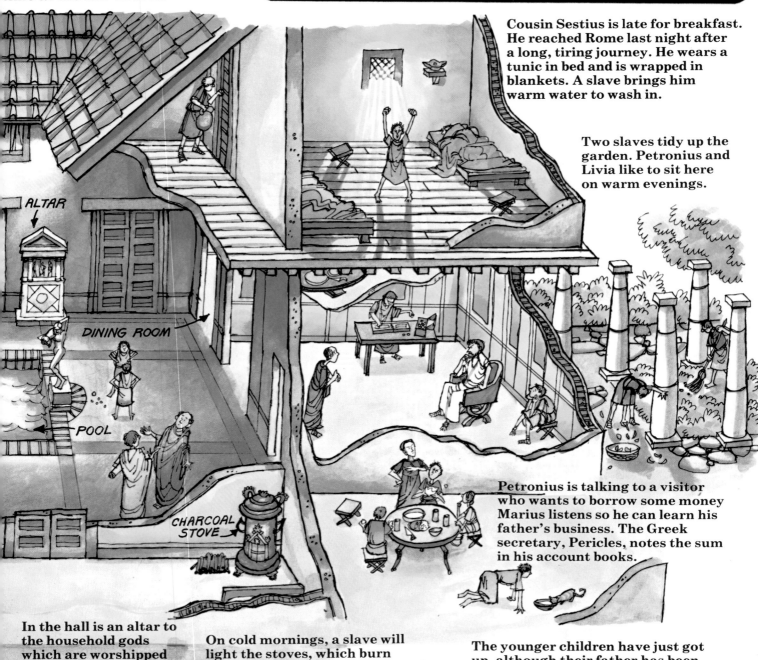

ALTAR

DINING ROOM

POOL

CHARCOAL STOVE

Cousin Sestius is late for breakfast. He reached Rome last night after a long, tiring journey. He wears a tunic in bed and is wrapped in blankets. A slave brings him warm water to wash in.

Two slaves tidy up the garden. Petronius and Livia like to sit here on warm evenings.

Petronius is talking to a visitor who wants to borrow some money. Marius listens so he can learn his father's business. The Greek secretary, Pericles, notes the sum in his account books.

In the hall is an altar to the household gods which are worshipped by the family.

On cold mornings, a slave will light the stoves, which burn charcoal—a special form of wood. There are no fireplaces or chimneys in the house, except for the cooking stoves in the kitchen.

The younger children have just got up, although their father has been at work for some time. They are eating a breakfast of bread, cheese and water, watched by Aunt Antonia.

Going to School

These boys are at a secondary school. They can go here after four or five years at primary school. They learn Greek and Latin grammar, arithmetic, geometry, history and all about the stars.

The boys are taught to speak and discuss in public. The Romans think this is very important.

Roman children go to school when they are about six or seven years old. Their fathers have to pay the schoolmasters. Some rich children are taught at home by private tutors who are often Greek slaves. Freed slaves start their own schools.

The schoolmasters are very strict and beat the children if they do not learn their lessons or are late. The schools start early in the morning when it is still dark. They end early in the afternoon so there is time for games or to go to the baths.

A BAKER GETS UP EARLY TO SELL NEW BUNS TO SCHOOL CHILDREN.

A BOY LIGHTS HIS WAY TO SCHOOL WITH A TORCH.

OIL LAMP

FAMOUS WRITER

THIS BOY FORGOT HIS LESSON.

SCHOOL FOR OLDER BOYS.

A slave takes a boy to school and carries his bag with wax tablets and pens.

Games

Roman children play lots of games in the streets when lessons are over. There are no school games or playgrounds for them.

Hoops are fun for rolling and jumping through.

Fights with wooden swords can be quite fierce.

BALLS ARE MADE OF LEATHER.

Two girls play a game called jacks with five small bones and a ball.

Stick and ball games have no proper rules so you can make them up as you play.

Wax Tablets

Schoolchildren write on boards spread with wax. They scratch words or sums in the wax with the point of a stick. They can rub out with the flat end of the stick.

Scrolls

Roman books are rolls of paper, called scrolls, and are written by hand. Each end of the roll is stuck to a rod. You have to unroll the paper to read each page.

Pens and Ink

People write on the scrolls with pens made of small reeds or of copper. The ink in the pot is a sticky mixture of soot, pitch and the black ink from an octopus.

FAMOUS THINKER

SCHOOL MASTER

WHEN IT IS DARK IN THE MORNING NO ONE SEES A BOY DRAWING ON A WALL.

THIS BOY IS RECITING A LESSON HE HAS LEARNED.

A GIRL WRITES ON A WAX TABLET.

Most schools are in the porches of buildings. A curtain stops people in the street from looking into the classroom.

At this primary school, boys and girls learn to read and write and do simple arithmetic. There are no books or paper to write on.

Every eighth day is a holiday. Then markets are set up in the streets and it is much too noisy to have lessons at school.

JAVELINS

Boys and girls learn to swim by holding on to bamboo floats.

Boys racing their carts pretend they are real charioteers.

Shops and Markets

The shops of Rome are small and dark. They are kept by the poor people and by freed slaves. In some streets are the workshops of craftsmen, such as weavers, silversmiths and shoe-makers.

Rich people go shopping only for clothes, jewels and other expensive things. They send their servants or slaves to buy food and wine and to take their clothes to the cleaners.

Meat, fruit and vegetables are brought from the gardens and farms outside the city. Noisy wooden carts carry everything to the shops and markets very early in the morning.

At the bakery, wheat is ground into flour. It is mixed into dough and baked in the oven.

OVEN

WHEAT

STONE MILL

FLOUR

DOUGH

PIG FED ON SCRAPS

The new loaves are sold at the bakery. There is no paper to wrap them in. The loaves have dents in them to make them easier to cut.

People meet in the noisy, dusty, and often smelly streets. They stop to gossip and hear the latest news of the wars and the empire.

Livia and Petronius are shown woollen and cotton material by the cloth merchants. Livia wants a new tunic to wear at a feast.

At the chemist's, a man has an ointment made of herbs, flowers and seeds put in his eyes. Ill people also buy magic spells.

ich Romans send their
lothes to special shops
o be cleaned. Men, called
ullers, spread them on
rames to bleach them.

Then the fullers put them
in tubs of water and a
special clay. They tread
on the clothes to get
the dirt out.

The clothes are dried
and folded and then put in
a big press to flatten
them. There are no irons
in Rome.

A slave collects the
clean clothes for his
master. He makes sure
the work has been done
well before he pays.

The Market

Today is a market day. Stalls, with
awnings to keep off the hot sun,
are set up in a city square. They
sell fruit and vegetables, meat and
fish. Musicians play to earn a
few coins from the crowd.

MUSICIANS →

A customer chooses a goose to be
cooked for a special feast. Usually
only the men slaves and servants
do the household shopping.

A butcher chops up a pig's head
in his shop. Only rich people can
afford to eat meat every day. The
poor fill up with cheap food.

This shop sells hot food for people
to eat in the streets or take home
with them. Many flats and houses
have no cooking stoves.

Afternoon at the Baths

Petronius goes to the baths in the afternoons when his work is done. The baths are not only for washing but are good places to meet friends, have business meetings and hear the latest gossip. Some men go there to do exercises, walk in the gardens or read in a quiet room.

Livia and her friends go to the women's baths or to these baths in the morning when men are not allowed in.

There are lots of baths in Rome. They cost very little and some are free. Only very rich people have baths in their houses.

Everyone leaves their clothes and sandals on the shelves in the changing room.

Some men live in the flats built round the cold bath. It is very noisy because the bathers sing, whistle, shout and argue.

This is the cold bath for cooling down after the warm bath and for swimming.

Hungry bathers can buy honey cakes from the pastry cook.

WRESTLERS

People can walk and talk privately in the cool gardens.

Dirty water goes into a huge tunnel under the baths. This drain has been dug under Rome and empties into the river.

14

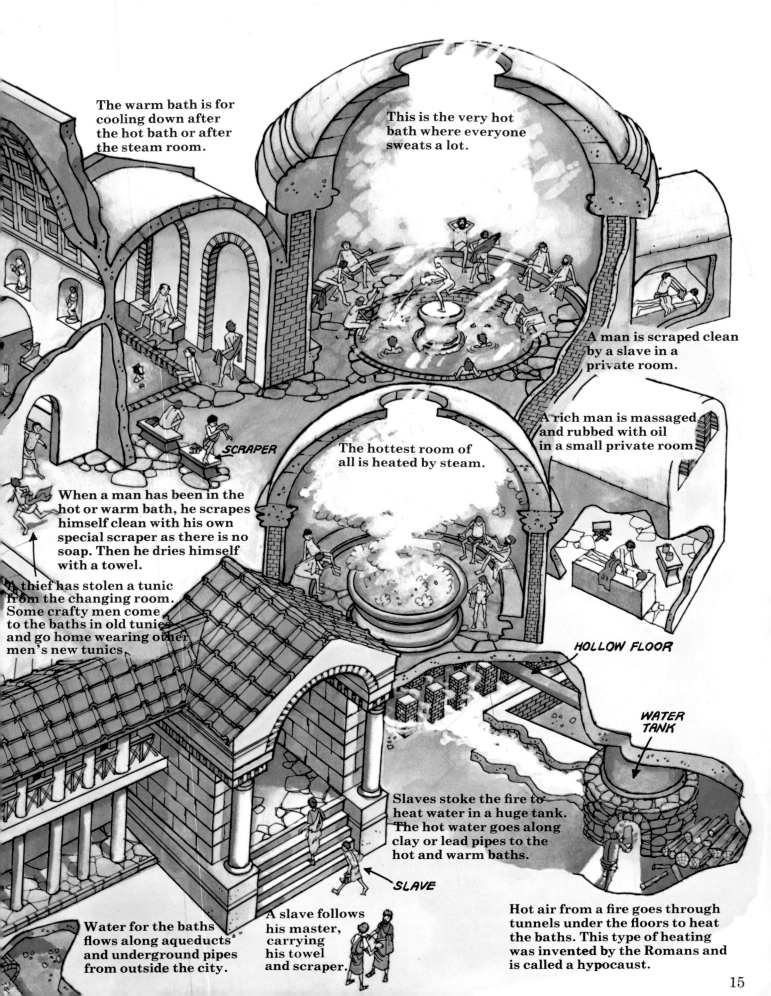

The warm bath is for cooling down after the hot bath or after the steam room.

This is the very hot bath where everyone sweats a lot.

A man is scraped clean by a slave in a private room.

A rich man is massaged and rubbed with oil in a small private room.

SCRAPER

The hottest room of all is heated by steam.

When a man has been in the hot or warm bath, he scrapes himself clean with his own special scraper as there is no soap. Then he dries himself with a towel.

A thief has stolen a tunic from the changing room. Some crafty men come to the baths in old tunics and go home wearing other men's new tunics.

HOLLOW FLOOR

WATER TANK

Slaves stoke the fire to heat water in a huge tank. The hot water goes along clay or lead pipes to the hot and warm baths.

SLAVE

Water for the baths flows along aqueducts and underground pipes from outside the city.

A slave follows his master, carrying his towel and scraper.

Hot air from a fire goes through tunnels under the floors to heat the baths. This type of heating was invented by the Romans and is called a hypocaust.

Gladiators and Charioteers

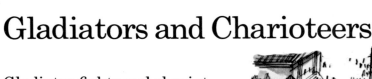

Gladiator fights and chariot races are the favourite sports of the Romans. At festivals and public holidays, people flock to the arenas and race tracks.

In the arena, prisoners and criminals are put to death. Some are attacked by hungry wild animals. Some are made to fight each other or are killed by the fierce gladiators.

At the race track, the emperor, rich men, noble ladies, poor people and children shout with excitement as the little carts speed round the course.

The biggest sports stadium in Rome is called the Colosseum. It can seat 45,000 people. A huge awning shades them from the sun.

Each of the 76 public entrances has a number. They are written on the tickets so people can easily find their way to their seats.

Gladiators are men who have been condemned to death. They are trained at special schools to fight and die very bravely.

Thousands of wild animals are brought to Rome for the fights. They are captured in parts of the empire as far away as North Africa.

Gladiators have different kinds of weapons to make the fights more exciting. The net fighter tries to dodge a sharp sword.

When he gets a chance, he flings his net over his enemy. He tries to tangle him up in it and stab with his fisherman's spear.

The wounded man begs for mercy. If the crowd gives the 'thumbs up' sign, he will live. 'Thumbs down' means he must die.

1

At the start of a race, the chariots wait at the starting line. Each charioteer leans forward, balancing the light, wood and leather cart with his weight.

2

The trumpet sounds, the starter drops his white flag, and they are off. Leaning back against the reins, the drivers beat their horses with stinging whips.

3

If the carts crash, or a wheel comes off, or a horse stumbles, the driver pulls out his dagger. Quickly he cuts the reins to stop him being dragged by the horses.

The Circus

Chariot races are held at the huge track called the Circus. Before the races start, priests and officials walk in procession round the track.

The horses race round the track seven times. The winning driver is given a purse full of gold and treated like a hero.

People bet on the drivers, choosing him by the colour of his tunic. They wave coloured banners and cheer to encourage him.

The turning posts at the ends of the track are the most dangerous places for the chariots and horses.

Only the best and luckiest drivers come out alive from a crash, called a 'shipwreck' by the Romans.

The charioteers wear metal helmets to protect their heads, and pads and leather bandages on their legs.

Building in the City

The city of Rome is always noisy with the sound of building. Old houses are pulled down. Sometimes they burn down or just fall down. New and bigger ones are built in their places.

New houses and blocks of flats are built by the poor people. Palaces, temples, bridges over the river, arches and aqueducts are paid for by rich people and by the emperor.

These men are building a new aqueduct. When it is finished, it will carry fresh water to fountains in the city where people get their water, and to the baths.

Stone for building is brought in big wooden carts from the quarries outside the city.

STONE BLOCKS

RUBBISH

Broken stone and building rubble is taken away to the rubbish dumps.

The rich people like the walls of their houses painted with pictur These are called murals. An artist paints on wet plaster while her assistant mixes the colours.

This man is building a wall of bricks made of baked clay. He lays them down carefully and sticks them together with mortar. This is a mixture of sand, mud and water.

MURAL

ASSISTANT

PIECES OF MARBLE

PLASTER   TILES

This man spreads plaster over the new brick wall.

These men are laying the floor. It is made of coloured marble, set out in a pattern.

18

The carpenters make wooden shapes to hold up the arches while the stones are put in place. The scaffolding is taken away when the arch is complete.

A crane lifts heavy stones up to the top of the columns.

WOODEN SHAPE FOR ARCH

← CRANE

SCAFFOLDING

Carving a Tombstone

A mason is carving a tomb stone for a rich man. Even poor people save up to buy tomb stones for themselves.

The stone is carved to show portraits of the man and his son. The pictures of tools show the man made coins.

Now the mason carefully cuts letters into the stone. You can read the man's name: P. Licinius Philonicus.

The stone workers, called masons, are always busy. They carve the pillars and big stones for temples, arches and other public buildings.

Tree trunks are sawn into planks by carpenters. They make the frames, doors and windows for houses.

CRANE

CARPENTERS

STONE MASONS

CARPENTERS

New tiles are put on the roof of the house. They overlap each other so that no water gets through.

MOSAIC FLOOR.   WET PLASTER.

A mosaic floor is laid in this room.

How to Make a Mosaic

BITS OF GLASS AND STONE.

WET PLASTER

The craftsman spreads wet plaster over a small patch of the floor and smooths it down.

Then he presses little squares of glass or stone into the plaster. Bit by bit, he makes up a coloured picture.

When the picture is finished, he rubs more plaster over it to fill in the small gaps between the squares.

Petronius Gives a Feast

The Romans spend their evenings at home. The rich give feasts for their friends and important people of the city. Poor people, who cannot afford oil for lamps, usually go to bed when it gets dark.

Tonight Petronius has asked some friends to dinner. All day, his servants and slaves have been hard at work preparing the food. You would think some of it is strange and tastes very nasty.

The poor people have cheap, dull food. Meat and fish are often too expensive for them to buy so they eat wheat cooked to make a sort of porridge. Sometimes a rich man will give a feast for them.

Slaves have carried this lady to the feast in a litter.

This guest is late but no one minds. There are no clocks, only sun dials and hour glasses in Rome, so it is hard to be on time.

Meat is roasted over an open fire. Sauces and vegetables are cooked in pots on a stove.

Everyone in the kitchen is very busy. It is hot and dark, and dirty with the smoke from lamps.

These two slaves brought their master to Petronius' house. They play dice while waiting until the feast is over. A slave brings them some supper.

Cooking

FISH WINE HERBS HONEY PEPPER

The head cook is making a special sauce for a meat dish. He pounds up the insides of fish with herbs, spices, wine and honey.

MARROWS BEANS PEAS ONIONS. LETTUCE

Two slaves chop up beans, onions, asparagus, lettuce and garlic. The vegetables will be eaten raw for the first course.

OYSTERS SNAILS

Live snails left in milk for two days have grown fat. One slave takes them out of their shells while another opens oysters.

Less important guests eat at this table. The food is not so costly and does not look so nice.

Musicians play a pipe and a string instrument, called a cithera, to entertain the guests as they talk.

This is the chief guest. He is so busy, he dictates letters to his secretary while he eats his dinner.

A man who has been to Britain tells the story of his slow, difficult journey. It took many months with lots of adventures.

A poet waits to recite some of his own poems.

This table is for the family and the most important guests. They have the very costly and nicest food.

Guests wash their hands between courses. They may slip food into their napkins to take home with them.

Everyone eats with their fingers from the big dishes carried round by the slaves. They can choose to eat the things they like best.

When they are full, the people drink and talk. They discuss such things as whether the chicken or egg came first; why men can see to read better when they are old; if wrestling is the oldest sport.

First Course

← OIL AND EGG SAUCE

STUFFED DORMICE

PEACOCKS' EGGS

The first course is a dish of stuffed and cooked dormice, stuffed olives and prunes, and peacocks' eggs with a sauce.

Main Course

CHICKEN

DEER

OSTRICH

DOVES

LOBSTER

BABY PIG

BOAR'S HEAD

All sorts of boiled and roast meat is served for the second course. The meat is sliced by the slaves as the guests do not have any knives or forks.

Third Course

FRUIT

HONEY CAKES

STUFFED DATES

The last course is a big glass bowl of fruit, a plate of dates and little cakes sweetened with honey. After this, the guests drink wine to each other's health.

21

Summer in the Country

During the summer, Rome is very hot and uncomfortable. Many people die of fever. Petronius takes his family and personal servants to his estate outside the city. He likes to spend some time in the country.

The estate has a big house, called a villa, in the middle of the farmland. There are rooms for the farm workers. The part where the family live is more grand and comfortable.

September is a busy time on the farm. The wheat, which ripens early in the hot Italian sun, has already been cut. Now the grapes and olives are picked to make wine and oil. All the food has to be stored for the winter.

At the end of the month, Petronius will take his family back to the house in Rome.

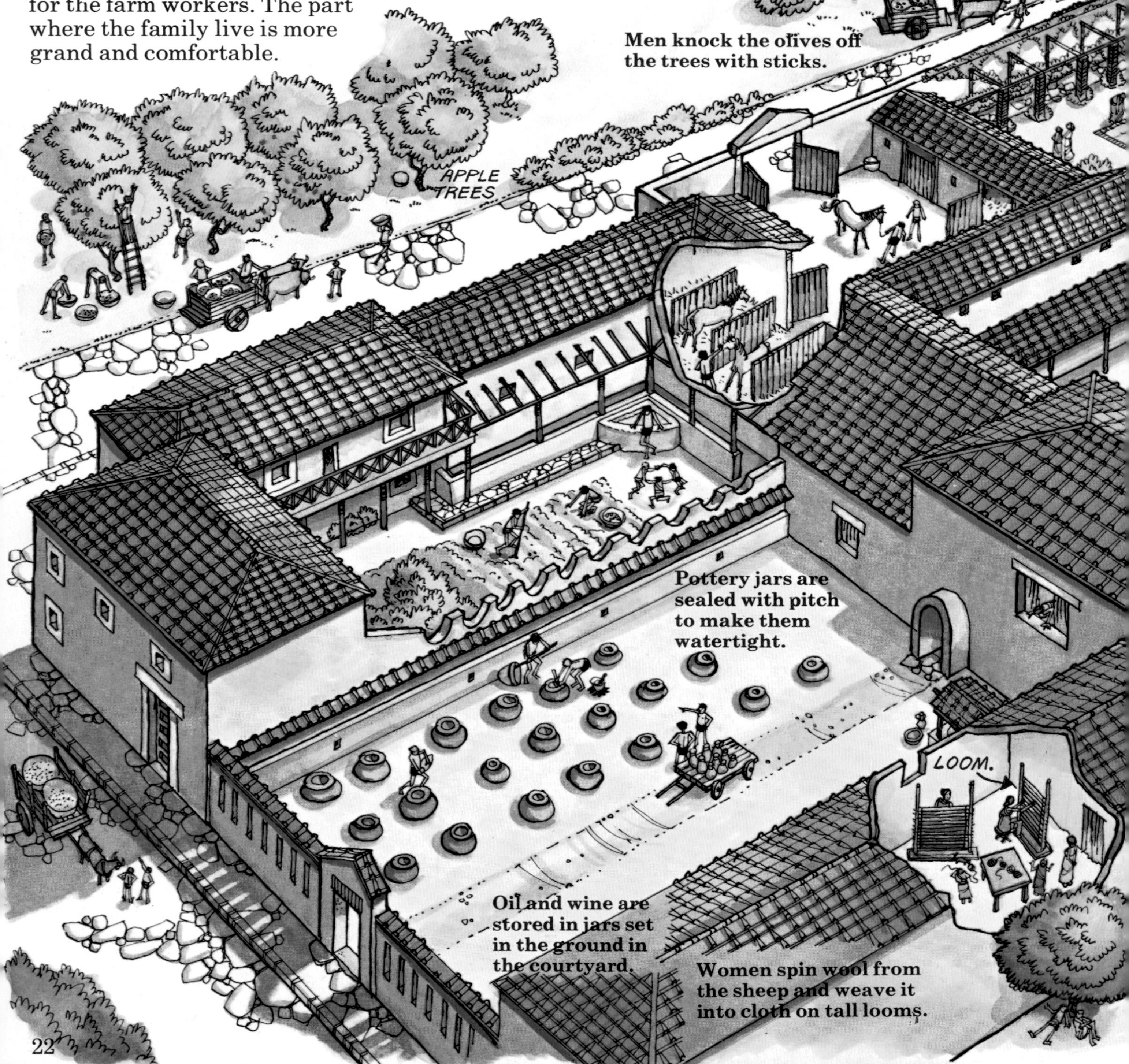

WHEAT STUBBLE.

SHEEP

Wheat stubble is burnt before the fields are ploughed again.

OLIVE TREES.

Men knock the olives off the trees with sticks.

APPLE TREES

Pottery jars are sealed with pitch to make them watertight.

LOOM.

Oil and wine are stored in jars set in the ground in the courtyard.

Women spin wool from the sheep and weave it into cloth on tall looms.

Paying the Rent

Some peasants lease land from Petronius. They pay rent for it with money, with the food they have grown, or with animals. The farm manager writes it all down.

Pressing Olives

When the ripe olives have been harvested, they are put into a screw press. Workers wind the handles to squash the olives and squeeze out the precious oil.

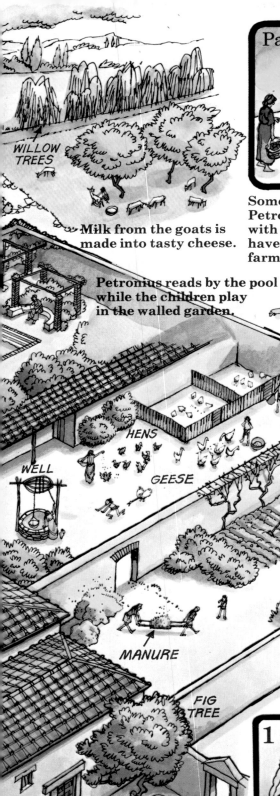

WILLOW TREES

Milk from the goats is made into tasty cheese.

Petronius reads by the pool while the children play in the walled garden.

PIGS

HENS

WELL

GEESE

MANURE

FIG TREE

A slave weaves baskets of sticks cut from the willows by the stream.

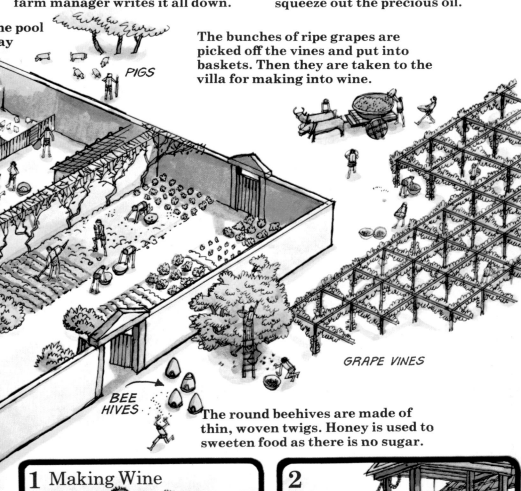

The bunches of ripe grapes are picked off the vines and put into baskets. Then they are taken to the villa for making into wine.

GRAPE VINES

BEE HIVES

The round beehives are made of thin, woven twigs. Honey is used to sweeten food as there is no sugar.

1 Making Wine

The grapes are tipped into a big stone trough. The men tread on them to squash out the juice. They have sticks to stop them slipping over on the mushy grape skins.

2

The grape skins are then put into a press to squeeze out the rest of the juice. The juice is put into big jars. It bubbles and foams as it turns into wine.

23

Marcus Joins the Army

Petronius' son, Marcus, is now 16 and is joining the Roman army. He has been sent to a camp, with other new recruits, many days' journey from Rome. Here he will be taught all the things soldiers have to do when they are fighting the enemy.

Thousands of soldiers live in the camps, guarding the frontiers of the Roman empire. The camps are surrounded by strong stone walls and some are so big, they are like towns. Cities often grow up round them as people move near to sell food and clothes to the troops.

At the camp, Marcus and other new soldiers have their names written down in the army record book. He swears an oath and promises to be loyal to the emperor. He will swear this oath again every year.

First Marcus is measured by an army tailor who will make his uniform. He will wear a tunic and armour made of metal and leather.

Next he tries on bronze helmets for size. They are lined with leather to protect his head.

Now the training begins. It will make the young recruits strong and good at fighting. They start with drill, marching twice a day, carrying spears and heavy packs.

Training

Marcus learns to fight by running at a target with a wooden sword. He and the other boys fight mock battles with swords and spears.

Horse riding is more fun but everyone laughs when Marcus falls off. There are no stirrups for his feet so he has to balance in the saddle wearing heavy armour.

The recruits learn to lock their shields together to make a 'tortoise'. This will protect them from enemy arrows and stones. But it is not easy for beginners.

The Fortress

When the soldiers came here many years ago, they built a strong stone camp. People now live near the camp and have put up shops and houses round the walls.

Part of the army has gone out on a long expedition. The soldiers left to guard the camp have time to repair the walls and grow vegetables in their gardens.

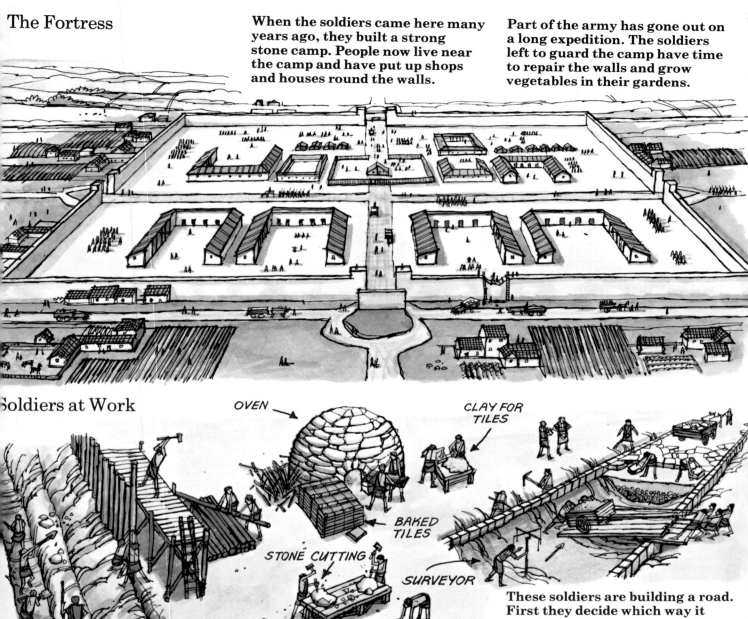

Soldiers at Work

OVEN

CLAY FOR TILES

BAKED TILES

STONE CUTTING

SURVEYOR

The recruits learn to dig ditches and set up wooden walls. When marching through enemy territory, they will make a camp of turf and wooden stakes every night.

Soldiers have to learn all sorts of things, like cutting and shaping stones, and making roof tiles.

These soldiers are building a road. First they decide which way it should go. This is the work of the surveyors. Then they dig a wide ditch and fill it with broken stone. On top go big flat stones. The road slopes down each side so that rain water runs off quickly.

1 Firing a Catapult

Today Marcus is taught how to fire a catapult. The officer watches as the soldiers wind down the huge beam with its sling.

2

Then a loader lifts a large stone into the sling. This can weigh as much as 30 kilos.

3

When they fire the catapult, the stone is flung into the air and lands about 30 metres away. It can easily smash holes in enemy walls.

Attacking a Citadel

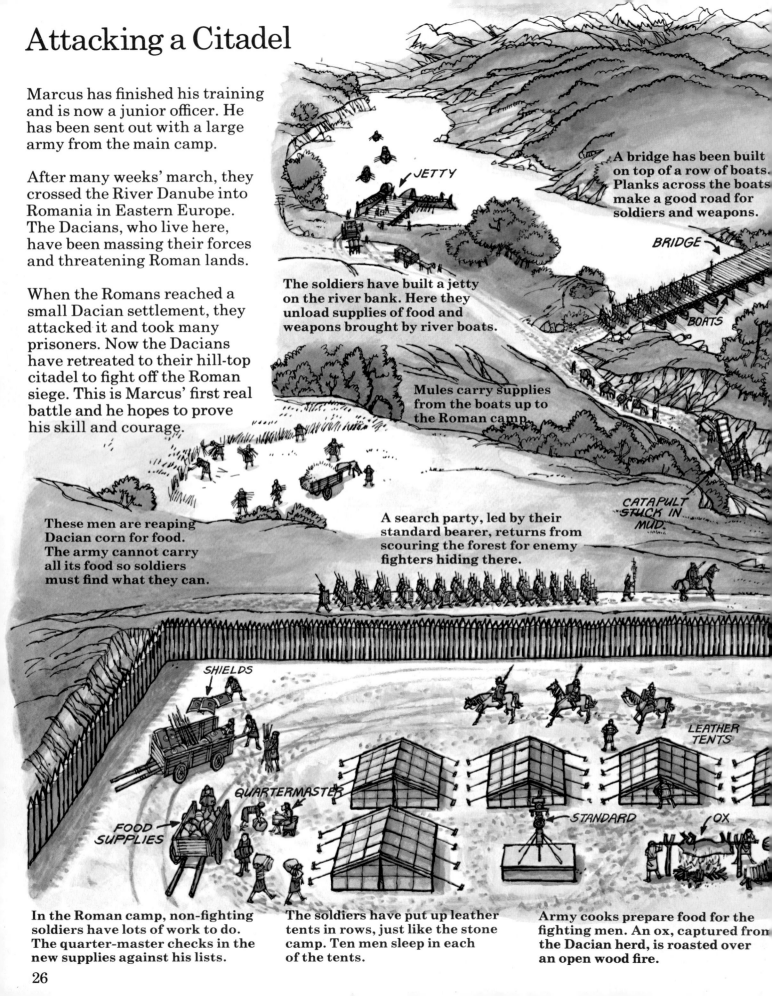

Marcus has finished his training and is now a junior officer. He has been sent out with a large army from the main camp.

After many weeks' march, they crossed the River Danube into Romania in Eastern Europe. The Dacians, who live here, have been massing their forces and threatening Roman lands.

When the Romans reached a small Dacian settlement, they attacked it and took many prisoners. Now the Dacians have retreated to their hill-top citadel to fight off the Roman siege. This is Marcus' first real battle and he hopes to prove his skill and courage.

JETTY

A bridge has been built on top of a row of boats. Planks across the boats make a good road for soldiers and weapons.

BRIDGE

BOATS

The soldiers have built a jetty on the river bank. Here they unload supplies of food and weapons brought by river boats.

Mules carry supplies from the boats up to the Roman camp.

CATAPULT STUCK IN MUD.

These men are reaping Dacian corn for food. The army cannot carry all its food so soldiers must find what they can.

A search party, led by their standard bearer, returns from scouring the forest for enemy fighters hiding there.

SHIELDS

QUARTERMASTER

FOOD SUPPLIES

LEATHER TENTS

STANDARD

OX

In the Roman camp, non-fighting soldiers have lots of work to do. The quarter-master checks in the new supplies against his lists.

The soldiers have put up leather tents in rows, just like the stone camp. Ten men sleep in each of the tents.

Army cooks prepare food for the fighting men. An ox, captured from the Dacian herd, is roasted over an open wood fire.

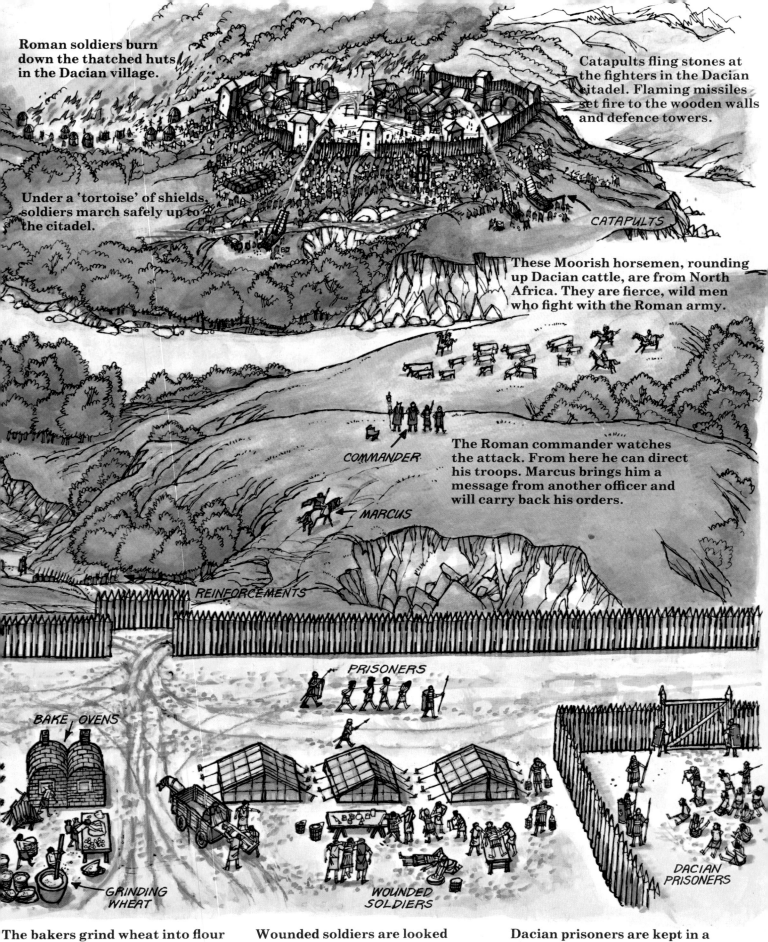

Roman soldiers burn down the thatched huts in the Dacian village.

Catapults fling stones at the fighters in the Dacian citadel. Flaming missiles set fire to the wooden walls and defence towers.

Under a 'tortoise' of shields, soldiers march safely up to the citadel.

CATAPULTS

These Moorish horsemen, rounding up Dacian cattle, are from North Africa. They are fierce, wild men who fight with the Roman army.

COMMANDER

The Roman commander watches the attack. From here he can direct his troops. Marcus brings him a message from another officer and will carry back his orders.

MARCUS

REINFORCEMENTS

PRISONERS

BAKE OVENS

GRINDING WHEAT

WOUNDED SOLDIERS

DACIAN PRISONERS

The bakers grind wheat into flour and mix it into dough. It is cooked to make hard, dry biscuits.

Wounded soldiers are looked after by army doctors. There is no hospital at the temporary camp.

Dacian prisoners are kept in a stockade. They will be sold as slaves when the battle is over.

27

The Roman Empire

Now move the flight stick on your Time Travelling Helmet and hover far above Rome. From a great height, you can look down on the map of the empire spread out below you and see how big it was a few years after your trip. It then took in most of Europe and surrounded the Mediterranean.

The capital city of Rome and other big cities in the empire were built near the sea and on rivers. This was so the food and all the other things needed by people living there could be brought by ships and barges. Look round the map and see where everything comes from and how it gets to Rome.

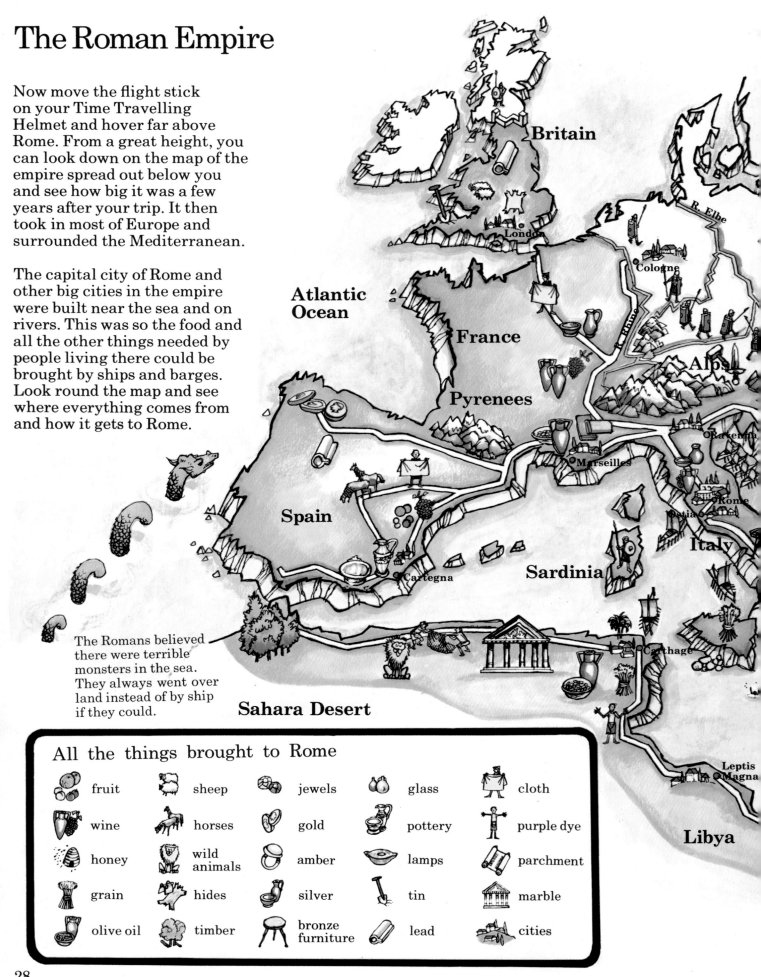

Britain

Atlantic Ocean

France

Pyrenees

Spain

Alps

Italy

Sardinia

London

Cologne

R. Elbe

R. Rhine

Marseilles

Ravenna

Rome

Ostia

Cartegna

Carthage

Leptis Magna

Sahara Desert

Libya

The Romans believed there were terrible monsters in the sea. They always went over land instead of by ship if they could.

All the things brought to Rome

fruit	sheep	jewels	glass	cloth
wine	horses	gold	pottery	purple dye
honey	wild animals	amber	lamps	parchment
grain	hides	silver	tin	marble
olive oil	timber	bronze furniture	lead	cities

The Romans called the people who lived outside their empire 'barbarians', which means foreigners. Some of these people did not live in cities, like the Romans, but travelled about. They moved in search of new land they could farm to grow crops of food and where they could graze their animals.

Sometimes they attacked the Roman frontiers to reach the land inside the empire. In the second century A.D., some of these barbarians fought their way right into Italy.

In the fourth century A.D., thousands of barbarians invaded Roman territories. They swept down from the north-east, destroying towns and cities, burning farms and killing the people. After they had captured Roman land, they settled down to farm it.

The Roman armies were driven back. The emperors could not get enough soldiers or money to fight the invasion, although the Roman people were taxed very heavily and were sometimes short of food.

The huge empire gradually grew smaller as the Roman armies lost their battles and were scattered. The barbarians even captured the city of Rome itself.

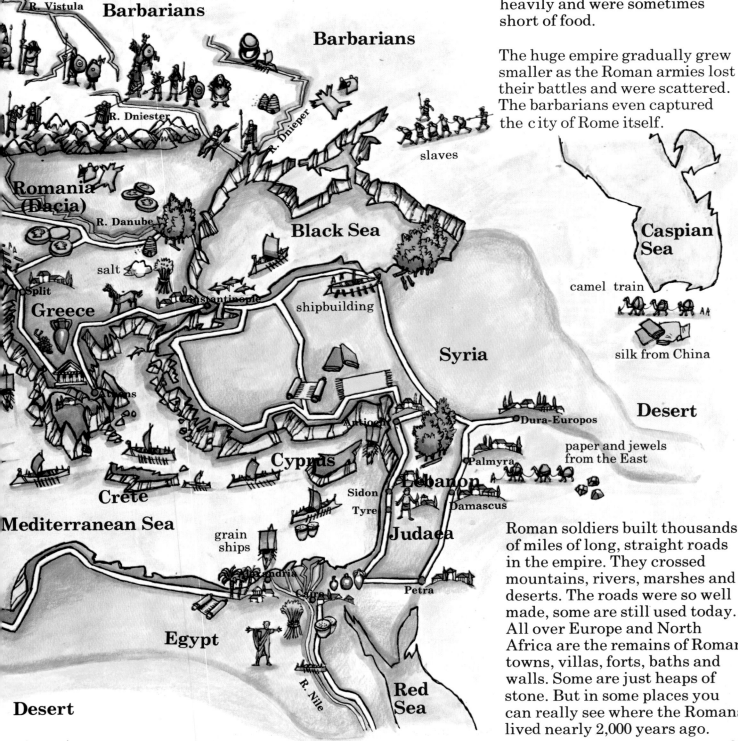

Roman soldiers built thousands of miles of long, straight roads in the empire. They crossed mountains, rivers, marshes and deserts. The roads were so well made, some are still used today. All over Europe and North Africa are the remains of Roman towns, villas, forts, baths and walls. Some are just heaps of stone. But in some places you can really see where the Romans lived nearly 2,000 years ago.

29

The Story of Rome

The story of Rome began in about 753 B.C. when some wandering people from Northern Europe reached a hill near the River Tiber in Italy. They built a village and settled down to grow crops and keep cattle and sheep. Soon the village grew and huts were built on the other hills. Later the villages joined up into a city and a trading centre, ruled by kings.

The people got rid of their king, in 509 B.C., and set up a republic, choosing two consuls each year to rule instead. The Romans fought and conquered their neighbours to protect their land. Gradually they captured more and more territory until by 250 B.C., they controlled the whole of Italy.

The Roman armies were strong and brave but, when war broke out with the people of Carthage, in 260 B.C., they had to learn to fight at sea. They built a huge fleet of fighting ships and soon won great battles against these fierce sea-going people, whose main city was in North Africa. The Carthaginians built a new base in Spain so they could attack the Romans.

In Spain, a young army commander, called Hannibal, built up a huge army. Many of Rome's enemies joined him and they marched, with 36 elephants, over the Alps into Northern Italy. He won many battles but the Romans cut off Hannibal's supply lines and stopped him reaching Rome.

The Romans landed in North Africa, in 204 B.C., to attack the city of Carthage. Hannibal sailed home to defend it but Carthage was defeated. Later, the Romans besieged the city and, in 146 B.C., completely destroyed it. The people were killed or sold as slaves.

The defeat of Carthage made Rome the greatest power in the Mediterranean. At home, the rich people lived in great luxury with slaves to work in their houses and on their farms. But they were greedy and paid people to elect them as state officials. In the provinces, some governors made their subjects pay huge taxes and robbed them.

Civil war broke out in Rome when two generals tried to grab power. One marched his troops through the streets, killing everyone he did not like. Then in 73 B.C. Spartacus, a slave, led a revolt. He escaped to Mount Vesuvius and was joined by 90,000 slaves. He fought off the Roman army until he was killed in 71 B.C.

Two generals, Julius Caesar and Pompey, struggled for control of the government. Caesar marched from Gaul to Rome but Pompey left for Greece. Caesar defeated Pompey's army there but Pompey escaped to Egypt where he was murdered. Caesar went to Egypt and made Cleopatra queen. After more conquests he returned to Rome.

In 45 B.C. Caesar became sole ruler of Rome. He used his power to bring justice to the people and planned to improve the city. But he had many enemies who feared he would become king. In 44 B.C. he was stabbed to death in the Senate.

Caesar's nephew and heir, Octavian, defeated the last of Caesar's enemies when he won a great sea battle against Antony. Antony, and later his friend, Cleopatra killed themselves. Octavian then became head of the state and its first emperor.

Octavian took the name of Augustus. He built up the armies to guard the Roman frontiers against invaders. He tried to conquer land north of the River Rhine but lost a terrible battle against German tribes. In the empire, people settled down to build new cities. The government built roads to bring peace and trade.

When Augustus died in A.D. 14, members of his family succeeded him. But the emperor was not a king and anyone who had enough support could come to power. In one year, there were four emperors, each put forward by different groups of soldiers. Later in the first century A.D., men who had not even been born in Rome became emperors.

In A.D. 117, Hadrian was made emperor because he was a good general. He strengthened the frontiers and built a great stone wall across the north of Britain to keep out the barbarians. In Judaea, the Roman army put down a revolt by the Jews and thousands were killed.

Early in the second century A.D. the empire reached its greatest extent. But the barbarians were attacking the frontiers. Southern German tribes were pushed forward by the tribes behind them and they swept into northern Italy. They were defeated but still threatened Rome's northern and eastern borders of the empire.

In the third century A.D., Rome's armies became a strong influence on the affairs of government. Many emperors were created by the troops and ruled for very short periods. The vast empire was very hard to control and there were many civil wars. Old enemies, such as the Persians, took the chance to regain land they had lost and even kidnapped and killed the emperor Valerian.

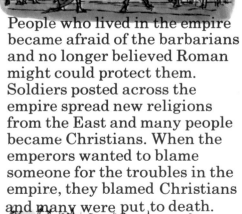

People who lived in the empire became afraid of the barbarians and no longer believed Roman might could protect them. Soldiers posted across the empire spread new religions from the East and many people became Christians. When the emperors wanted to blame someone for the troubles in the empire, they blamed Christians and many were put to death.

For a few years, the empire was saved by the emperor Diocletian. But there was not enough money to pay the armies needed to fight off the invaders.

The next ruler, Constantine, won a battle to become emperor with the Christian sign on his standard. He made Christianity the state religion in A.D. 320 and set up a new capital in the east, called Constantinople, after him. The eastern, and stronger, half of the empire was ruled from there. It held back outside enemies until 1453 when it was overrun by the Turks. But the barbarians invaded the western half of the Roman empire and, in A.D. 410, they sacked Rome. A barbarian made himself ruler of Italy in 476 and the empire was destroyed.

After the barbarians overran the empire, many Roman things remained. The barbarians became Christians, and Latin— the Roman language—became the language of the Church. The languages now spoken in France, Spain, Italy and Portugal all developed from Latin and there are many Latin words in Dutch, German and English. Roman ideas of law and justice have been adopted by Western law and many cities have copied the Roman style.

31

Index

Altars 9
Aqueducts 6, 15, 18–19
Ambassadors 6
Army,
   camps 24–5, 26–7
   Dacian 26–7
   Roman 24–5, 26–7, 29, 30–1
   training 24–5
   uniform 24

Bakers, 10, 12
   army 27
Baths, 14–15
   water for 15, 18
Bread 10, 12
Books 11, 23
Building 18–19

Carts,
   farm 5, 6, 12
   racing 17
   toy 11
Catapults 25, 27
Chariot races 16, 17
Cheese 9, 23
Chemists 12
Circus, the 17
Clothes, 8–9, 12, 13
   cleaning 13
Colosseum 6, 16
Cooking, 4, 6, 13, 20
   army 26–7
Cooking stoves 6, 9, 13, 20

Dacians 26–7, 28–9
Drains 6, 8, 14

Emperors, 6–7, 30–1
   palace 7
Empire, Roman 6, 7, 28–9, 30–1

Farmers 5, 22–3
Feasts 20–1
Firemen 6
Flour 12, 27
Food 5, 6, 9, 12–13, 20–1, 22–3
Forums 6
Fruit 5, 6, 13, 21
Fullers 13

Games, 16–17
   children's 10–11
Gladiators 16
Grapes 21, 22, 23

Honey, 20, 21, 23
   cakes 14, 21
Horses 5, 16, 24
Houses 5, 6, 7, 8, 18–19, 22, 25
Hypocaust 15

Ink 11

Julius Caesar 7, 30

Lamps 8, 10, 11, 20, 21
Litters 6, 20
Looms 22

Markets 6, 11, 13
Masons 19
Meat 4, 13, 20, 21, 26
Mosaics 19
Musicians 13, 21

Pens 11

Olive oil 22, 23
Olives 21, 22, 23

Priests 7, 17

Races,
   chariot 17
   children's 11
Rivers,
   Danube 26
   Tiber 5
Roads 4, 25, 28–9
Rome,
   baths 14–15
   buildings 6–7, 18–19
   city of 4, 6–7
   shops 12–13
   sports 16–17
   story of 30–1

Senate House 7, 30
Schoolmasters 10–11
Schools 10–11
Scrolls 11
Shops 6, 11, 12–13
Slaves 8–9, 10, 20–1, 29
Soldiers 4, 5, 24–5, 26–7, 29, 30–1
Spices 6, 20
Staging posts 5
Swimming 11

Taverns 4
Temples 6, 7, 18
Tiber, River 5, 6–7
Togas 9
Tombstones 4, 19

Vegetables 5, 6, 13, 20, 25
Villas 5, 22

Water 4, 8, 14, 15, 18
Weaving 22
Wheat 12, 20, 22, 26, 27
Wine 20, 21, 22
Writing 11

Further Reading

The Roman Army by Peter Connolly
(Macdonald)

Imperial Rome by Alan Sorrell and
Anthony Birley (Lutterworth)

Republican Rome by E. Royston Pike
(Weidenfeld and Nicolson)

Great Caesar by Plantagenet Somerset Fry
(Collins)

The Ancient Romans by D.A.W. Dilke
(David and Charles)

First published in 1976
by Usborne Publishing Ltd
20 Garrick Street
London WC2E 9BJ, England

© Usborne Publishing Ltd. 1976

Printed in Belgium by
Henri Proost, Turnhout, Belgium

The name Usborne and the device
are Trade Marks of Usborne Publishing Ltd.